27 Threats
to Everyday Life

poems by

Anne Holub

Finishing Line Press
Georgetown, Kentucky

27 Threats to Everyday Life

Copyright © 2023 by Anne Holub
ISBN 979-8-88838-135-9 First Edition
All rights reserved under International and Pan-American Copyright Conventions. No part of this book may be reproduced in any manner whatsoever without written permission from the publisher, except in the case of brief quotations embodied in critical articles and reviews.

ACKNOWLEDGMENTS

Much Appreciation to Journals Where Some of These Poems Appeared:

"Thrown" and "Traffic" in *The Mississippi Review*
"Bears" in *New Plains Review*
"Insomnia" and "Dive" in *West Trade Review*
"Feeder" in *Great Lakes Review*
"Wildfire" in *Clackamas Literary Review*
"Seizing" in *the tiny journal*
"Mesothelioma" as "Mesothelioma Sestina" in *Plainsongs Poetry Magazine*
"Mudslides" in the *Western Humanities Review* as the runner-up in the 2022 Mountain West Writers Contest

I would like to thank my husband, Dan Snedigar, for his ongoing support and patience in every bookstore aisle. Also thank you to friends who helped read this manuscript and gave such excellent advice and feedback, including (but not limited to) Wendy McClure, Rosamund Lannin, and Claire Zulkey. Much appreciation and gratitude to the Open AIR Artist Residency at the Flathead Lake Biology Station in Montana where several of these poems were written or conceived. Finally, thanks to sleepless nights, anxiety, scraps of paper with half-legible notes, and the internet: without which I wouldn't have nearly enough to worry about.

Publisher: Leah Huete de Maines
Editor: Christen Kincaid
Cover Art: David Schalliol
Author Photo: Larissa Cook
Cover Design: Elizabeth Maines McCleavy

Order online: www.finishinglinepress.com
also available on amazon.com

Author inquiries and mail orders:
Finishing Line Press
PO Box 1626
Georgetown, Kentucky 40324
USA

Table of Contents

Wildfire 1

Bears 2

Flash 4

Seizing 5

Mudslides 6

Thrown 7

Insomnia 8

Virus 10

Night Driving 11

Feeder 12

Traffic 13

Plaque 14

Elevation 15

Bees 16

The Sugar 17

Ticks 18

Air Conditioner 20

Mesothelioma 21

Run 23

Neighbors 25

Pines 26

Tinnitus 28

Bridge 30

Trigger Fish 31

Apnea 32

Nicotine 33

Dive 34

For my mother,
who came to all the readings
and would have bought two dozen copies.

Wildfire

Sunrise in fire season, and we've already choked back smoke
    from the window panes.
This is the time the wind quiets, the heat not yet a force that can lift.

Help us to understand the speed of it all,
As if a conflagration could be easily mapped, marked, clocked—
A radar gun aimed at the trees cresting the dry hill behind the house.

The dogs cough to be let outside. You know where they're heading:
Bellies flat in the crawlspace, slowly
Digging their way under the porch tinder to moan.

This is the history of the Camp, before that, the Okanogan Complex,
Before that the summer Yellowstone burned, the Rattlesnake, and
    Mann Gulch
—the one they jumped and lost.

Call this a warning or a watch, call it manmade or an act—
What brings more danger:
The color of the sky in morning or the ash on the car where we can
    write a name?

Who can we pray to when we don't dare light a candle? When
    summer rain
Would bring lightning and kindle?
What can we do but dig in the dirt and hold the line?

Bears

      There is a bear over the hill.

Skinny from winter and
milk sore, with claws and fur full of pine
and the smell of last fall's blind gorge.

Hyperphagic in October, she'd crossed
the highway after dark,
eyes reflecting the moon.
She was pregnant then. Even
she knew it. Could tell she needed
more food than a few rose hips
that soured her rough tongue.
She raided the orchard for fallen peaches,
ate cherries left to wither. Scraped
the roots of skunk cabbage
between her teeth and
smelled for viscera left rotten.
She scavenged deer,
plucked porcupines roadside.
She waddled.
She reveled in her fat—
licked blood between her claws like jam.

      There is a bear over the hill.

After the last night of frost she dug into
a wide trunk and slept. She
laid her wide head against the
same soft wood she'd grubbed out
and smoothed with her pads.
Over her head the snow began, it clung
barked and westward facing.
It drifted over her dreams—they called it a blanket.
It was quiet.
She missed months of sunsets.

In the spring was the cubs' insistence. The
twins rolled inside her as the ice cracked—
tugged her insides like the buoy chain.
Snapped her slumber.
They forced her eyes awake, her lips
curled back into a Yes.

    There are three bears over the hill.

The drifts cleared. They emerged
with a newfound love of wind and the
sound of the lake lapping rocks.
They learned to run. To fall in the sand.
She licked their faces clean, showed them logs and
beetled bark. The larches' greening
heralded the fat bulbs of glacier lily,
the sedge, the cow parsnip. They dug cold earth.
Scooped mice into their mouths,
played with them like toys
and crunched small bones that
popped and gave way.

I know there is a bear over the hill.
A slightly darker shape in the shadow of the cabin,
she smells the door at night
tests its strength like a strange key
and wakes me from sleep.

    She is hungry, and she is not alone.

Flash
    Big Thompson Canyon, 1976

a gathering:
the talk of drought and the never-pending rain
the men rap their knuckles and hum falling sounds

*

you stand camera-ready, delicate and glassy
the way you write the curve of your letter f
feels somnambulant (dangerous in the dark),
periscopic, your eyes in unnatural light

water easing under our feet
is more than just an accumulation / a warning
we already know, there are ways to drown—
in wheat, in a coat or hat of your father's

*

one hand finds the smooth wall,
wants to feel the rock
and define the distant growling

if light can flood through the afternoon
why is the canyon floor so dark
what is there to run from

Seizing

Outside each
window, a view
of needled tree limbs bent
against the panes.
How much weight
you bear
between your teeth?
Can we manufacture
the time we spend
together into something
that bleeds meaning? Our bodies—Look.
Hands often lack
sincerity. Take that from your mouth.
Look here. Replace your unutterable
fears with names
for the old mountains behind your house,
their worn slopes much
softer than you had anticipated.
Look me in the eyes. The trees,
the trees are shaking.

Mudslides

We check the weather
like we're going to leave the house soon.
Barometric pressure changes—
a feeling of mercury rolling in the chest and
the limits of lung expansion
        —time wasted boiling eggs
in the mountains—a
literal watching the pot.
The dog shifts under the table
where he's braced for a storm only
he can smell.

Watch the cities rise up on hillsides
where the houses have a better view.
Watch them fill in the valleys so
there's something worth falling on
after the rains come. After the fire season ends.

We feel inside our pockets for a worry stone.
There's a seam ripped somewhere and
a thread dangling loose. Worry it like a tooth.
The dog growls in his sleep. He warns
slick ash holds no water. It

skims the surface, builds dams
with debris found loose and rootless.
They say a landslide fails when it begins.
The telephone poles begin to lean in
to hear us better.

The door is stuck tight.
The rain has stopped.
Someone is knocking.
  *

Bodies in the mud, pressed like
shells
into fossils.
La conchita. Little shell.

Thrown

These ruddy hills stitched thick with horses. Rope-bridled and mudded, their eagerness to refuse a jump is something like the screeching hesitation of car wheels, dopplerized and cunning, a momentary loss of equestrian control leading to distinct injury (the opening of legs too far and a sense of falling out of rhythm) indescribable except for the snapping sounds: an absence of heartbeats—a pressureless universe worse than any overly-weighted existence. In your chest like a collapsible chair: a fear that rusts through summer. It was not that warm, the 27th of May, but there was a shivering beneath your hands. You could have heard the prelude from the hoofbeats, but you never would have landed. You would have pounded your frame and towered above that which held you suddenly still or flown to safety. What becomes of wasted energy if it does not fall back into the mouth? What of the discordant sirens—their atonality more than you can press to the flowers with your lips? I wonder how your body feels in the bath, if your arms still float up from your frame. You must be tired of hearing the word *wait*, a pause like the wind.

Insomnia

I.

the dark in which I know
your body and your reaching arm
the dark of what was said
into the dim frame of room—our clothes
at the foot of the bed now a lingering pressure
between our feet, and the streetlight left
knocking at the pull-shade, a swinging
shaft of stained light too sure to be the sun,
searing across the wall a slim diagonal—
as if your voice could be so light
my back, so burned that I rub against the sheet,
try to wear my skin and sweep the char away
to confuse my nerves with friction, steady,
pin down through the night and remember
the low sounds making their slow descent

II.

>Are you awake, I have to ask who will have me now I've given away my plans for nights deep with breaths, how could you forgive how I fill each hour pretending sleep, all the time spent half-shut and fluttering, perhaps too drawn to the sunrise, beating there against the window or seeking the bright in light bulbs, holding everything until it burns.

III.

Don't think the scraping rain remembers
earlier, at twilight, the dim ridge above the trail
and the dog, vibrant, flushing the impossibly round birds

who always cry out like something sharp stuck
in the gullet—don't worry about the sounds
that dry skin scrapes along your back, the hair's
sharp memory, a mistake you laugh through every time you think
about what you could have done and
your hands over your mouth—as if speaking
of it were only the beginning of your fears.

IV.

    This is not a proper way. These fists cannot find much comfort when clenched. They stiffen into flowers, grow brittle against the skin, behind the tongue, the throat. With compulsion, and some sense of numbers, I roll a lolling ankle and warm the sheets with elliptical friction. But this is not the way to burn through dawn. There is nothing to be afraid of, some might tell you, then point out the bears in the sky. The clouds have moved in and I cannot count the stars for seeing.

V.

before me there was still   doubt
does it burn   does it leave a mark
there is still the proof
what degree of   whole   is enough
and empty   we empty out
behind our eyes   mouths open
from the black   say
the stars are broken they snap
curling against fire   held in our laps
like strands of hair   say
some nights are gladly spent

Virus

I press and press
fat pills, again, again, against
the roof of my mouth. Hitch
my head back and hope.

I am drowning inside where
two lungs would drink themselves dry
like drunks at the bar.
I'd order a round
if my throat wasn't already closed tight—
a red road torched a brushfire,
cells charcoaled
discarded downward and
even ice chips like matchsticks.

I am thick with air I can't breathe—
clouded, seeded with pills that won't dissolve.
Everything clicks in shades
of gray as pixels disintegrate
in synaptic misfire, treacherous cells
now incubators of cytokines:

A virus that would first split me in two
to divide, and divide, and divide.

Night Driving

I still remember
the way he drove at 4 a.m.,
the silver streamline blurred black,

hidden in fog so thick we could just see the shape of
deer pressed tight against the shoulder, unaware
just how close and how deadly we were.

I felt each state line in jolts
as asphalt changed to fair-weather concrete tinged dark
the tires licking the red stone—tasting.

He listened to the radio while I feigned sleep,
the dial plunged into the depths of AM
where the air was too thin for talking,

voices panting a code while lights hugged
the curves of aching guardrails, a straining slingshot
around anonymous truck drivers, flannel-clad and bleary.

A pause for refreshment. At the seatbelts' snap we rolled apart,
clung to the windows and sailed away
on waves too brittle for eye contact.

But we couldn't get far, no denying
the codes that linked us by hair tips and a finger prick—
our sparks, like metal on metal, contained the inevitable crash.

Feeder

At first sight, wrens appear hungry enough
to strip the bark, or even paint from cars
if only their beaks were so sharpened, could slough
sure rust from some abandoned nail, some scar
unclaimed and left for Tuesday's collection.
They scrape the grass and drink from one cupped leaf,
ignore the bread I toss, decide to run.
They scatter, schooled like bright fish brought north, left
to weather drifting snows, to keep their warmth
hid under brightly colored fins, now air
beneath their wings, now snowflakes piercing forms,
their red, dramatic blood: their rage declared.
They fill their throats with stones, then lift their eyes
to what can still just serve as borrowed sky.

Traffic

The rocks we took from Montana are beginning to grey, which always happens when they become dry and then indistinct. I can't tell you which river they came from, though I roll them under my thin shoes with a motion they're used to. I can't make out the markers here, but I can see three men in a circle on the median. They smoke. They wear jackets with mountain names and look like they know where they're going, how long it will take to get there. It's too simple to wonder how many cars make a mile. I should calculate the distance from here to home, figure alternate routes and gas reserves. I should wonder where we left the map, why it didn't seem like something that needed saving. There is too little movement here and I wonder if everyone is playing at something, if they're rolling stones where I can't see. I get out of the car and stoop to the road, warm and confused at our stillness, the length of our stay. I kneel and pick at the black tar-stones, peer down the stripe of highway. The men talk of construction and blasting ahead, they move their hands like small explosions. The cars line up too easily, their lights now two still rivers, one red one white, too like veins and arteries, this road an arm slashed and left to bleed.

Plaque

A sore spot in your mouth
and a blooming
web stuck
to your teeth
on your elbow
where the road turns
against your heart.

The acids
dissolve
you bit by bit.

Elevation

What you think is a mountain
is actually cloud
will disappear from view
one foot after another

This crest comes with a chance of sudden
snowfall / crosswind / switchbacks
and a feeling you might be falling
a feeling in your head you can't explain
can't wish away or clear
with a deep swallow towards the base of your throat
a small growing lump at the base
of your skull
at the top of your spine
that you can't see on your own
won't wish others to touch.

We seek the equilibrium of sea level
zeros balanced
bubbles no longer heading to shore or sky.

Is neutral flight that which doesn't feel like flying at all?
Are you falling if you never hit the ground?

Bees

The shock of it all.
Feet on your face, the sudden unwelcome
attention to your eyes and
hairs around your ears.

This wasn't what you expected,
We're not suited
were not veiled and wedded
to the idea.

It's not enough to be tolerant
to be and let bee
to whisper—Bee, out
as they hover before tasting.

It's never enough to be sweet,
to be not sweet enough,
to be shaped like a flower
though you too bleed from your stems.

It comes on like a blush—
small hairs on your arms lifting.
A fainting spell.
A clutch of the heart until

nothing is left and
we cannot stop their stings.

The Sugar

A run, a tear in your skin that refuses to heal while you explore it for hours in the dark (you call out) that could be someone outside your door (dark thought) and with your nails try the paint from the window joints and call out to the seams that run from their tracks like dark shapes needling over the hills, like slivers beneath your heel, some spurs, the pace moved there from the chest   there is no time for standing   your palms and wrists swing in an upward motion, open, two open arcs (sure paths) bracing the curve of hillsides, the heavy water and rock, the bending effortless, as when you moved without regarding your feet or hands

Ticks

And what is it that you should remember
about size and shape of the wound, the mouth's name, the color,
a ring around it a red penumbra—*erythema migrans*.
Do we wait for the slow droop around your cheek
and a fever, or was it an itch?

(You remember a teacher placing one on top of a penny, for scale.
Lincoln's face replaced with a fat squirming body. A whole summer
you imagined your pockets full of insects, 25 for two bits.)

Their heads thrust into skin for a meal, like
a child bobbing apples in a tub. Red stuck to their chins,
their bites a rose-colored indentation
in the flesh, a sometimes rash, a shaking.

And how should you remove this wriggling seed from your skin?
Your mother once pinned you and accomplished the feat
with a quick touch of a hot match head,
try the flick of a nail and a rusted tug like
you're unlocking a door with an unfamiliar key.
Hold your arm steady in the good light and try not to scream.

Sweating by the bathroom window you cradle a phone and a tweezer
and wish you had listened better, not put your head to the warm ground,
remembered to seal the edges around the camper's air conditioner vent
or was it the culprit the old shirt with the split seam? Can we blame
something so efficient in its design?

Scrolling, you learn the females lay thousands of eggs.
You imagine an eight-footed legion under your leg creases,
fattening behind your ear, snug in your hairline. They
set up camp for the night and you wake up weaving in the mirror.

Undisturbed, they swell and fall off like limp grapes
—small legs waving a drunk refrain.
Between meals, they cling where they can,

use their mouth's sweet bacteria to synthesize vitamins and wait.
The females are larger, they create their own B9, folate,
mate and lay eggs somewhere soft and warm.

Sure of nothing except a metal taste rising in your mouth,
you grasp it along the flat torso, exhale in a burst
like a tea kettle, repeat your own name. And pull.

Air Conditioner

Held high above with nothing
more than optimism
and a brick.
There's a hum
and a drip—
a mystery of rainfall
or airplane spit.
Slow grind of fan
with the occasional
fly massacre,
or dust mote,
or unfortunate bee.
Is it negligence
to leave the machine
purring against the windowsill—
a place for the cat and its sunbeam?
Is it a tragic final resting
place for tape ends and cups and a misplaced
earring? The forgotten whatever
you threw
to the window's edge
when you last undressed
in the dark?

What will we hear
before the cord gets
tangled around our feet?
Can we smell
the plastic frame shattered
around a gap of brick.
The cold air dissipating
in a burst of Freon
and bone.

Mesothelioma

They said it wouldn't burn.
But we could feel it like a blanket
smothering us from the inside/out.
They said it was safe.
It wasn't enough to just send us to gather it in the mine,
every day we brought more up, in our breath.

Men stacked fish-deep in an elevator, sucking shallow breath—
worried their dark thoughts will ignite and burn.
The weight of the darkness like a blanket
in your pockets, wearing out
two holes where your hands hid—safe
from your shaking eyes, as you shuffle into your shift, their mine.

That's a funny thought. That it's *mine*,
not theirs. But your breath
is only yours. Like a match you burn
against the cup of your hand, an old blanket
of stars—familiar as a thumbprint. Set out
to find something new, and you'll lose what's safe.

That's what she says every time you're home safe.
"Praise God, and let the devil know you're mine."
You can feel her hot breath
on your neck as you sleep, as your thoughts burn
against the light, like moths birthed when you fold the blanket,
try to set things right in a square, smooth them out

and make something better than what sifts out
of the rail cars, into what sits dusty in a safe.
You can tell them at the mine
about your children, their sweet breath
whistling as you inhale every day like a burn
across your lungs, a blanket

over your chest. Time weighs like a rotting blanket
and stones you can't piss out.
It holds you down with the irony that it keeps others safe
(but not from dust you dig from the mine).
It wasn't your windows fogged with winter breath
but your lungs that will slowly frost and then burn.

They sold your breath in the mine,
abandoned you like a babe in a blanket and called it safe.
The doctors cannot take it out. You can only sit and burn.

Run

The man with the baseball hat
nods when he passes you,
heading the other direction from your house.
You listen to his footsteps to make sure
he continues walking
doesn't turn and follow you into
the shadows past alleys
and garbage cans where you saw
discarded clothes
a purse, opened
its contents spilled to the damp.

You listen despite the silent earbuds
you wear to discourage conversation.
The armor you wear in layers, to hide your shape,
the keys you hide in small pockets
sewn for no other purpose,
the hair you tuck up uncomfortably,
sticky against the back of your head,
to prevent a handhold from behind.

Emergency details are carved on a bracelet
(silver, not gold—lower your worn worth).
You suffer from:
anxiety, asthma, depression,
bouts of gastrointestinal distress,
fits of sudden crying,
the inability to leave your bed some days,
torments in evenings
when you break into a run
heading home from the train
in the twilight dark, your brain screaming,
your heart pumping the slick taste of adrenaline
into the back of your mouth.

They say: don't run in the dark,
you can't be seen.
But someone is shooting strangers
at ten o'clock in the morning now
and you can't hear footsteps
over the blood rushing through your ears,
but you hope you can hear him run
behind you.

Neighbors

The chandelier shudders
under the repetition
of feet,

heat in crescendo,
so far past combustion
that the floor sags
beneath their feet.

Another word,
swallowed sentences and
a bruise to her
skin,
tender as a dropped apple,

the shock of two bodies
and the smothered music
they're making,
first,
        a low, hollow sound,

then stillness—
as if gravity was
a theory.
Not a law of attraction.

Pines

Above me the tall trees are swaying
and I look to see what could possibly be
leaping from their tapered stems,
what grabs hold of sticky tufts of green
needles and sheds them
haphazardly
onto the forest floor below.

But there is nothing
that I can see
except what was wind
and what is the threat of rain.
      The shadow of where a tree once was
now is only the wake of bending. And sky.

The force of this restlessness loosens
the oldest pinecones
sheds bark and scales left
to flutter downwind
from where gravity would pull them—
      like some feather of a lighter thing.

    (we pretend they are light, that they are nothing)

The more unfortunate
branches snap with abandon, they
would rather choose a clean cut of saw
than this jagged edge of wrathful difference.
      We would shout with our sharp teeth bared and ready.
But they fall when told.
We cannot prevent this.
That is more terrifying than the falling.

The trunks are meant to be pliable,
by design are intended for vacillation.
They don't pick a side. Can never
be relied upon for casting the deciding vote
or choosing a risk over a quiet night alone.

They anchor their toes around
stones slowly rolled here by glaciers. Will not
be told new stories. Cannot
accept any ending but the one they were
provided in their original packaging.
The same story translated in cracking bark.

Unbox this: pierce to open.
See how sap creams hard to amber
in the light under the clouds.

The trees sway above our heads.
We cannot help but fear their
swift sounds: knocking.

Tinnitus

That hum isn't a truck
coming over the railroad bridge,
but the steady chewing
of honeycomb under construction
behind walls
a thrumming unsettled and shifting.
It grows louder on hot afternoons
like a wonky ice cream truck—
        its song gone sour.
Something isn't right here.
But we're too used to the vibration
like a radio left on low overnight so you can sleep.
The bees winter over in between
slats of soft wood.
They suck their feet,
shake pollen from their pants
and rehearse steps and directions.
Would you rather map this path
like a heart carved on the back of my hand
or a sapping tree in thaw?
Would the cutting hurt if you knew the destination
was to be sweet?

Focus your eyes through the screen door
past the cracked glass on a diesel truck.
See that flag? It's red for a reason—a warning.
Down South they'd call that shade pokeberry or clay, a stain,
something that sets the dog growling at the
faded lilac bush in the night.
What shadows are we carrying
back home in our sog-bottomed boxes
full of earwigs and candle nubs.
What are we keeping all this around for?
Leaning tennis trophies against the wall and a basket
of half-finished potholders we should have
left by the side of the road.

These boards have become loose and the paint
is dripping at the seams. (The window aprons mildewed,
split and the rain sloughing down.)
Hammer a nail into the swarm
and see who stings first.

Bridge

I. In

No one dared tell the river that Spring arrived.
Its brackish banks still sudsed with a frozen crust
of salt and slick duck feathers, lost trees bent
grey with coal dust, all protesting equinox.
The river insisted it was still winter—
the worn stones preferred the slow pace below ice
while cars hurled themselves across
its thick white bridge like children
rushing past the darkest house on the street.
Hold your breath, cross your fingers.

II. Out

Ahead, a musty truck kicked up enough road grease
that your wipers threatened revolt,
resolved to paint over a smear so dense
that you couldn't see the shore
until your wheels clapped the last joint
and you pitched headfirst into Maryland, surprised
that the road hadn't collapsed
under the weight of it all: the truck, your car, and
the idea of the river hidden below, growing so large
that nothing could escape the water, not even its name.

Trigger Fish

You learn how to breathe first,
as if so many years above sea level
aren't enough to help you understand
how to suck air in and push it out again.

Then taught not to panic—
how your lungs will swell
if you come up too fast,
bursting one by one like balloons.

Below, once you're weighted down,
once you've proven you can remove
your mask and replace it,
you're free to float horizontal, to tilt,

to stick your hand in various
holes and see what comes out.
Beware of fire coral—its scratch
a burn against your skin that water cannot quench.

Watch for spines, keep your gear from dragging
the ocean floor and stirring up silt,
be careful of caves you cannot exit,
and getting separated from your buddy.

And the *Balistidae*,
all stripes and pouts.
They attack hands and face—the fleshy bits
an invasion of their brood,

your ears all but picking a fight beside your mask,
your blood filling the wash,
and sharks nurse nearby.

A panic you cannot escape
swimming upwards only whetting
their appetite and rage.

Apnea

Some nights, when
you should be asleep
I wake and wait
for a sign that you're still breathing.

You don't stir as I lift my head,
press my lips tight to stifle my own gasp,
grip my hair so tight, tears floating like
boats dodging icebergs at night.

Do I want to know the answer?
I can only just make out your face turned away
and I hear—what? A wheeze from the dog, or
the furnace turning over in the night.

I stamp my ear in the gap of air above your chest,
my head hovering, the hairs on my cheek testing the air,
hoping to feel a breath, a tremor
from the back of your throat—rapidly cooling in the night.

You just lay there like an abandoned bay.
Is there life behind your lips
curled tight—a wet rag
caught out in a winter storm?

If I wait, will your lungs press up,
or even now do your breaths sink
like drowning seals caught
beneath a sudden ceiling?

Is your body any warmer
when you're awake?
Can you catch your breath, just once,
and still wake up dead in the morning?

Nicotine

In the cabin, the logs absorbed the smoke,
in the rings—*tertiary amine*, meaning, derived from ammonia
sharp receptors counting
binding to the tree cuts, cleaned / polished hard
and smoothed like the stairs,
sock buffed rings snagged
on the sharp grooves
of pinecones set by the fireplace
unraveling
a basket of tinder
alert like smelling salts
and the sound of thunder
at 3 a.m. like a backfire
        —exhaust, leaded
        not unlike a gunshot, not unlike a gun
in its menace, which is why I tie bows on the
gun rack by the front door. The door by the fireplace, where
the smoke pinches cheekward,
curls around clocks
and stains the log chinks
black, lazing up the flue
that drips down soot when it rains.

This is why I can't sleep:
the rain coming down inked runnels and
filling up the small boat tied for safety,
to the lamppost out back.
a landmark
a landmine
a tow line
a water line.
The lake flooding and the creek's to blame.
Nicotine and pianos, thudding in your chest.

Dive

What handsome lies
we tell ourselves in summer—
slick patches darkening under arms,
between legs caught too long
against vinyl seats.
Released from a long drive (the promise of destination)
        with sucking sounds like a cap opened slowly.
Like some foreign filament stuck between
your teeth that you just can't give up on.

Gazes adjust from above the water
to catch shadow from a darker patch of light
        —how deep is it here?
Could we leap from rocks
and blow small bubbles skyward until our feet
land silted in the crushed sand
atop the bodies
of ancient phytoplankton that fell too far below the surface
those unlucky ones that
caught the wrong current that
couldn't reach the light.
If we dove
headfirst would we break our necks?
What caution are we
throwing to where
our mothers stand
trying not to look concerned?

We should hold a rope and ease in,
form a human chain and shuffle feet (one/two)
until someone kicks a lump of something / no one / no body
wishes to find.

www.ingramcontent.com/pod-product-compliance
Lightning Source LLC
Chambersburg PA
CBHW022122090426
42743CB00008B/968